Stars in the Lake

Gayani Gamage

BookLeaf Publishing

Presentation by *BookLeaf Publishing*

Web: www.bookleafpub.com

E-mail: info@bookleafpub.com

ISBN: 9789357443227

First edition 2023

I dedicate this book to the passion I have for writing and everyone who helped me to live in this world with love, faith and hope.

Falling

Drops of water
Heavy and hard.
Tears or rain...
No one really knows
Steps or missteps..
Falls or stumbles..
Moving on and getting up
Raining in or shining sun
Drops will fall
till death do us part

Hiding spot

Mountain and clouds
plays a game of old times
hiding till they are seen
seeking till they are tired
The sun
The moon
The Stars
The lake is good
They say, we believe

Annoyance

Throw those sticks
up up into the sky
far far into the forest
fetch and bring
game or not

Lockdown

Locked out and locked in
Tears in and smiles out
Two corners of one house
Locked down or locked in

I Need You

Hope was the weight that held it altogether
Faith and love were the soldiers of conqueror
Deep underneath, the roots that inspire
Lovers were the starts, fallen for desire

Thorns

Sleeping under the thorny bushes
Waiting for those falling petals
Needing comfort in this undergrowth
Bleeding heart with a rose in hand

Sun

It broke early
It shone brightly
I closed all doors
The window let it in
I closed myself
Nights were better

Lost

Running through the forest
Avoiding those hedges
Creatures of large and small
quantities were not my scare

Moon

It moved
Everywhere
from room to room
Here to there
In every corner
To every corner
till the all mighty
power of earth
roared and shone
still no where to hide

Fog

The sight, the look, the outlook
The view, that picture, that photo
shadows of grey and white
covering the lens
Those eyes, the lens, the view
Not allowed
No access

Growth

It stood still
naked and bare
the bark is nothing
they say its laid bare

Slow and long
Time takes its time
Sky is open
Seasons of change

Small but strong
leaves and their shoots
Flowers not yet
No need not now

Green and yellow
Colours of mellow
Dance with might
Wind in the willows

Happiness

Endless, endless, endless times
Rolling in and out of memories
Remembering and reminding
Waking up and staying up
Digging deep into the mind
Searching and the corners
Searching the pits
Finding nothing
as its all laid bare

Raindrops

Rain leaves the drops
Memories crawl inside
Sun beams and destroys
Faces are buried beneath
End of long leaves
It remains, it shines

Offspring

Lakes, mountains and clouds
Born beneath and above
Earth, Moon and Sun
It's a wonder never a surprise

A squirrel, a lark or a cub
Sounds of nature as a hub
It's in nor it's out
No speaker plays this sound

The cry, the need, the want
The nature gains and it gives
Breeding offspring of its own

Evening

Checked out, thrown out
Gates locked out, day is done
Harness on to the ride
Horses gallop
Chickens cluck
Packed in coops
Packed in tight
Darkness reigns
Starts not bright

Moon in lake

Perfect and mild
The dawn of night
Nothing too bright
Nothing too loud
Peaceful and calm
Creatures not in sight
Only a light
that shines
in the lake

Street life

Streets are full of sounds
Vendors and workers alike
Smells of food and flowers
Creating moments of life

Something from the sea
Something from the hills
Something from the ground
Coming altogether
Selling life and lives

Generations

Older the wiser
No one really knows
Younger the stronger
Elders wink and smile

Past, present and future
Ages all aligned
Sitting on this bench
life after life

www.ingramcontent.com/pod-product-compliance
Lightning Source LLC
Chambersburg PA
CBHW062112140826
49812CB00058B/1315
9789357443227